Q-Learning: Mathematical Foundations and Applications

Dedicated to my Mom and Dad, and the rest of my family

Chapter 1:
A Brief Introduction to Machine Learning and Artificial Intelligence

The first ever conceptualized version of the computer was pioneered by Charles Babbage in the 19th century, where he proposed the Analytical Engine, a mechanical, general-purpose computer that could be used to perform any form of calculation, computation, or optimization. He theorized that the computer would ideally be able to be explicitly programmed; it would be able to take direct commands from the user and produce a tangible output.

Babbage never saw his idea come to fruition; however, Babbage's designs laid the groundwork for computer parts that are commonplace today: the arithmetic logic unit, integrated memory, and basic programming structures like conditionals and loops.

Ada Lovelace, another computer programmer who worked closely with Babbage, wrote the first "algorithm" in tandem with the computer designs that were put forth by her colleague.

During the 20th century, there was a wider transition in the computing world from mechanical to electronic computing. With the invention of the vacuum tube, electronic computers such as the ENIAC and Colossus occupied entire rooms and consumed large amounts of power and were used extensively throughout World War I and II. In the years following the war, the transistor was invented in 1947, which led to smaller and more energy efficient computers. Transistor counts in modern computing chips now range from millions to even billions.

The 1960s and 70s saw the development of integrated circuits and the first microprocessors, which led to the miniaturization of the computer and saw personal computing and business computing become even more prevalent. Early computers in this era such as the Apple II and the IBM PC marked a distinct technological revolution.

As networking and the Internet grew more complex alongside computers, the ambition to create machines that were able to emulate human intelligence grew as well.

From a technical standpoint, the terms "artificial intelligence" and "machine learning" have become so ubiquitous that it's important to step back and analyze what these terms really mean in the context of our contemporary technology.

Artificial intelligence (AI) is the broadest of these buzzwords; it refers to any computer program that emulates human thought and decision-making. AI could simply be executing an if-then statement (e.g.

if the temperature in the house is below a certain amount, turn on the heater), which mimics a human thought process and can be translated into a computer program. AI can also encompass topics that can perform more complex tasks, such as classifying an image as a cat or a dog.

The primary thing to realize is that artificial intelligence, in its simplest forms, must be explicitly programmed based on the information that we humans already know. Unlike humans, however, primitive AI is unable to synthesize new ideas or make connections between topics like we are able to. This fact, therefore, limits the breadth of problem-solving that AI is capable of.

Computer programs gain the ability to make intelligent decisions and connections independently from pre-programmed instructions in a subset of AI programs known as **machine learning** programs. The types of programs that machine learning can solve are much more varied: clustering and customer segmentation, simple image classification, fraud detection, customer retention and churn, etc.

Machine learning in and of itself is a general term; there are a couple of sub-architectures and paradigms within it that will prove valuable to understand.

The first and most common machine learning paradigm is known as **supervised learning**. Supervised learning gets its name from the fact that the machine learning model is "supervised" with labeled training data; the model gets data (e.g. an image, number, etc.) as well as its corresponding label and uses this to be able to make predictions about future data by making generalizations about the current data.

Let's take an example: we want to investigate the relationship between the number of bedrooms a house has and its listing price. We would create a model by feeding in labeled data, which would be a large number of houses and their corresponding number of bedrooms and listing price, and the model would create a system to translate the number of bedrooms to its approximate cost. We would then be able to plug in a random number of bedrooms into the model and get an approximate price range. Note that using numerical outputs to get an approximate numerical output can also be referred to as a *regression model*, due to its creation of a regression line or a line-of-best-fit.

We can improve this model by taking into account other factors that determine a house's price, such as square footage, the number of bathrooms, location, etc. These additional characteristics that we are adding to our model are known as *features*. Generally, if you include more model features that are readily available and practical, your model will become more comprehensive and precise. However, it also takes more time to collect all of these features and hand-label the data, so it is important to have a proper balance of features in your model.

A common term which you may have heard thrown out which falls under the category of supervised learning is known as a neural network. A neural network is an architecture used within a subset of supervised learning known as **deep learning**. Neural networks are applicable for complex problems due to their brain-like structure; interconnected computational units known as *neurons* and the mathematical links between them store decision-making capabilities.

As seen in Figure 1, neural networks consist of an *input layer* which maps the input data to a specified number of neurons, *hidden layers* which do all of the underlying processing, and finally the *output layer* which details the final product/conclusion.

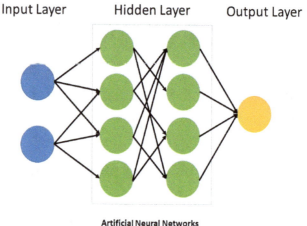

Input Layer   Hidden Layer   Output Layer

Artificial Neural Networks

Figure 1: Neural Network Diagram
Image by TseKiChun, licensed under CC BY-SA 4.0, via Wikimedia Commons

A common example of a problem in which neural networks can be applied: training a model to classify handwritten digits (0-9) given corresponding training examples. Large-scale datasets, such as the MNIST dataset containing over 60,000 training examples and 10,000 test examples, would be a strong choice.

A common analogy used to explain the purpose of neurons and their connections is assigning each neuron an attribute of the data itself. For example, when writing the number "8," the neuron(s) which represents the upper and lower loop of the symbol are likely far more important than the neuron that dictates the thickness of the letter's written stroke. In this sense, the neurons dictating the loops of the "8" have a greater *weight* than other neurons.

In addition to its weight, neurons also have another computational parameter known as a *bias*. Although the weight of a neuron scales with the magnitude of the input data, the bias is an additional translation independent of the input data that can help add extra nuance and simulate functional cognitive learning. Furthering the point of cognitive learning, neurons also have an *non-linear activation function* that transforms the data analogous to the non-linear formation of synaptic connections in the brain.

The values of the neurons in a neural network are initially random. The accuracy of a neural network with respect to the training data can be modeled by a function known as the *loss function*. Minimizing this loss function involves finding the minimum of a multivariate function, which involves a process known as *gradient descent*, where partial differentiation is utilized to make small changes in individual parameters (i.e. a single weight or bias) until the minimum is reached. Gradient descent informs how the neuron values should be updated; the process of continuously updating these values is known as **back-propagation**, a cornerstone algorithm of deep learning.

Other supervised learning algorithms which you can feel free to read into that may be of interest include: support vector machines, random forest decision trees, k-nearest neighbor algorithms, among others.

Unsupervised learning is another common machine learning paradigm; however, it is often employed for more abstract and complex tasks which can't rely on the supervision of humans for data labeling and training. Rather than being trained on human-defined features and characteristics, the machine learning model itself discovers patterns and makes predictions without any explicit human guidance. This makes it applicable for use cases where the data scientists and analysts don't know much about the data themselves and how to interpret it.

Due to the lack of labeled data, unsupervised learning models are essentially incapable of data classification itself. However, they can take a multitude of data points and *cluster* them (Figure 2) based on intrinsic similarities which the model itself discerns; this makes it applicable in cases such as custom segmentation and recommendation systems, anomaly detection, etc.

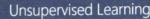

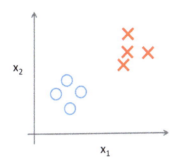
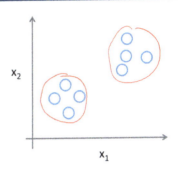

Figure 2: Supervised vs. Unsupervised Learning
Image by Pouya Tahmasbpour, licensed under CC BY-SA 4.0, via Wikimedia Commons

The final and arguably most prospective machine learning paradigm is **reinforcement learning**, a substantially different approach to the aforementioned methods. Rather than training a model to classify or learn patterns about a set of defined data, reinforcement learning is a more abstract technique that is based on making optimal decisions.

Similar to greedy algorithms, reinforcement learning uses trial-and-error in the learning process similar to the process which humans use. A more rigorous definition of reinforcement learning will be described in the next chapter. For now, it's important to realize that reinforcement learning is based on taking the most optimal actions to maximize the cumulative "reward" which is obtained as a result. The reward can either be explicit or implicit.

A common example of reinforcement learning in action is the learning process of robotic vacuums such as Roomba. When a Roomba is first introduced into a new environment, it doesn't have any prior training knowledge which it can use to inform its path. Instead, it starts out essentially moving at random, eventually transitioning into a trial-and-error approach where actions that lead to better, faster paths are more optimal.

Chapter 2:
Reinforcement Learning and the Markov Decision Process

Now that the basics are out of the way, let's get into some of the theoretical knowledge required to understand reinforcement learning, which will be pivotal later on for our understanding of Q-Learning.

Reinforcement learning can be simplified into interactions between an intelligent **agent** and the surrounding **environment** in which it resides. In most game theory-esque cases, the goal of the agent is to repeatedly roam around and explore the intricacies of its environment. The way we quantify the value of an agent's exploration is its collection of various **rewards** that it may find throughout its journey.

Similar to back-propagation, which is applied to continuously improve neural networks in their training, the agent takes multiple **episodes** to refine its understanding of its environment and maximize the number of positive rewards that it collects.

Each location or physical place in which the agent can be in in the environment is known as a **state**. Mathematically, they are simply represented with the character s.

Each state is unique; it represents a distinct form or instance of the environment that the agent is in. The agent, therefore, needs to be able to move between various states for greater discovery and, more importantly, a greater chance of getting rewards!

The way an agent gets to another state is by taking, arbitrarily, a specific **action**. Actions can be represented with the character a. Now, there are usually several actions that an agent can take when in a specific state. When the agent begins its training, it essentially chooses actions at random. However, as more and more training episodes occur, the agent begins to make generalizations about which actions are good and bad, and specifically chooses strings of what it has determined to be good actions to hopefully get better rewards.

Once the agent eventually reaches a new state, the agent may or may not receive a reward. This is an important note: not every state has a corresponding reward. In most cases, rewards are sparsely distributed across the array of possible states, and it will take many different state-action pairs to ultimately find a reward.

Below is a diagram of the agent-environment reinforcement learning paradigm:

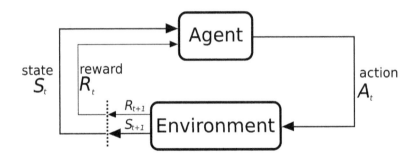

Figure 3: Agent-environment paradigm
Image by EBattleP, licensed under CC BY-SA 4.0, via Wikimedia Commons

We see in Figure 3 that upon taking action A_t, the agent moves from state S_t to state S_{t+1} while collecting the reward R_{t+1}, which then signals the cycle to repeat.

Quick side note: in some cases, the action that an agent takes doesn't always do the same thing when in the same state. For example, if in state s and action a is taken, there may be a probability of 0.8 of transitioning into state s_1 and 0.2 probability of transitioning into state s_2.

In this sense, we can call this type of problem non-deterministic, or **stochastic**. This property of stochasticity is typically favored in mathematical representations of reinforcement learning (particularly Q-Learning) because it is more generalizable and encompasses **deterministic** learning within it. Deterministic learning means that every action taken in a state has the same resultant state after. Furthermore, in most real-world cases, stochastic representations are favored due to their inherent ability to handle complex situations.

Stochasticity requires a **probability distribution function** of states, actions, and rewards to describe all the possibilities of a state-action pair. This can be expressed as:

$$P(s', r|s, a)$$

where the next state s' and the reward r are probabilistically dependent on the results of the previous state s and the action a that is taken within that state.

So, let's quickly summarize. The agent starts out in a particular state and can take quantifiable actions to change that state, which depends on whether or not the problem is stochastic or deterministic. Although new states don't necessarily guarantee rewards, the agent traverses through multiple different states collecting both positive and negative rewards throughout each training cycle, or episode. As the agent performs more and more episodes, it cognizably generalizes whether certain states and actions are harmful or beneficial to the agent, and takes measures accordingly.

This entire section has been describing one of two types of reinforcement learning systems, **value-based** reinforcement learning. The other reinforcement learning system is called **policy-based**. These two systems have fundamentally different approaches for how they extract the namesake **policy**. The best way to think about an agent's policy is its strategy; it dictates how exactly the agent should act in specific states to be able to get the most rewards over time.

Now, value-based reinforcement learning is more implicit compared to policy-based reinforcement learning. It works by simulating many different state-action pairs to estimate the value of different actions in different states. To do this, the system progressively creates a **value function** that takes a state and an action for an input, and produces the approximate reward as an output. From that information, the policy can be extracted by always selecting the action that maximizes the value function.

There are two types of value functions, one of which takes just the state as an input, and one that takes the state and the corresponding action. These can represented as $V(s)$, the **state-value function**, and $Q(s, a)$, the **state-action-value function**. Hey, I wonder if that Q-function will be important later...

Policy-based reinforcement learning, on the other hand, is much more direct and doesn't involve the creation of a value function. To learn more about it, you can read Chapter 7 later on.

Okay, that's most of the prerequisite knowledge required to understand reinforcement learning, and by extension, Q-Learning. Now, let's dive into some underlying mathematical assumptions and principles that help to bind together all of these ideas together.

First, let's introduce a topic required for the feasibility of Q-Learning, the **Markov property**. The Markov property is an assumption under Q-Learning that the future state of the agent is solely dependent on the current state and action that the agent takes, and not the history of state-action pairs that it has taken before reaching the current state. Therefore, this means that the decision-making process can be effectively modeled using only the current state and action, making it much less computationally complex.

Mathematically, the Markov property states that the future state s_{t+1} and future reward r_{t+1} are solely dependent probabilistically on the current state s and action a. This can be expressed as:

$$P(s_{t+1}, r_{t+1}|s, a)$$

Now, let's further extrapolate this idea by introducing the **Markov Decision Process (MDP)**, which also includes the theoretical knowledge seen earlier in this chapter. The MDP is a mathematical framework to describe reinforcement learning problems in an environment. It rigorously defines the flow of states, actions, rewards, and the transition model between different states. Let's look at each individual aspect:

The state is in the set of all possible states in the environment. For clarity sake, lowercase letters represents explicit values and uppercase letters represent the random set which they are a part of. This can be written as:

$$s \in S$$

The action taken is in the set of all possible actions resulting from the current state, so:

$$a \in A(s)$$

The reward r that the agent obtains is of course in the set of all possible rewards. However, to be rigorous, it is also important to note that the rewards themselves must be contained within the set of all real numbers:

$$r \in R \in \mathbb{R}$$

This qualification helps keep the complexity of the problem statement simple and not require tools with further complexity.

We noted in our definition of the Markov property that $P(s_{t+1}, r_{t+1} | s, a)$ could be used to define the probabilistic transition model from one state to another. While this definition still holds true for the MDP, its important to distinguish that the time at which current/future states take place is discrete:

$$t \in \{0, 1, 2, 3, ...\}$$

Q-Learning and most other reinforcement learning methods work on discrete time steps to episodically update values, so time is kept discrete for simplicity.
We mentioned the policy earlier as essentially representing the agent's strategy in picking an action when in a particular state. The MDP helps to inform that policy, which provides a probabilistic model for choosing the next action. We can represent the policy stochastically with:

$$\pi(a|s)$$

An alternative way to write this if the environment is deterministic is:

$$a = \pi(s)$$

Naturally, we want our policy to be as strong as possible so we can accumulate the most reward. The accumulation function is also known as the return, or G_t. One extra complexity added to the return function is the optional **discount factor**, represented with γ $(0 < \gamma \leq 1)$.

The discount factor prioritizes recent rewards over rewards that are accumulated later, which prevents the robot from wandering around aimlessly, and will be explained further in visual explanations of reinforcement learning. The return function can be expressed as:

$$G_t = \sum_{k=t+1}^{T} \gamma^{k-t-1} R_k$$

Expanding this out:

$$R_{t+1} + \gamma R_{t+2} + \gamma^2 R_{t+3} + ... + \gamma^{T-t-1} R_T$$

Upon first glance, this may look intimidating. Let's take a closer look. We see that the discount factor compounds itself with the next time step's reward, which makes sense. We want the agent to prioritize rewards now so it doesn't waste time, so this prevents the robot from looking around forever for rewards which it may not even find.

We see that the expression stops at $t = T$, which is known as the **terminal state**. Now, in other definitions of the MDP, you may see this as an infinity sign, making it a true MDP. However, in most practical cases, it's better to think of MDP's as a conclusive process, which means they could also be given the name Finite MDP.

That's a lot of mathematical groundwork and assumptions out of the way. Just to recap, must assume that the agent is in an environment which follows the Markov property and functions with the bounds of a Markov Decision Process.

Typically, we also usually assume that we have full understanding of all states and the transition model (again, $P(s_{t+1}, r_{t+1}|s, a)$, and that all data can be fit in a tabular form.

Typically, the state-action pairs and their relative values are stored in a tabular form, as will be explained further later on. Therefore, it is typically implied that the number of state-action combinations can reasonably be fit within a tabular data structure.

We will now take all of this knowledge and use it to finally introduce the topic of this book, Q-Learning!

Chapter 3:
The Bellman Optimality Equation and conceptualizing Q-Learning

If you recall from last chapter, we defined a state-action value function that can quantify the relative value of an action taken within a particular state with a number. An instance of this function is represented by $Q(s, a)$.

In order to write this Q-function, we must pool in a lot of the previously learned content, which we'll get into later in this chapter. For now, just think of the equation as just a function which is able to episodically calculate and update changes to the various Q-values.

It's usually best to think of storing these Q-values as a table, with the rows and columns representing the states and actions, respectively. The **Q-table** could look something like this:

Q	a_1	a_2	a_3	a_4
s_1	$Q(s_1, a_1)$	$Q(s_1, a_2)$	$Q(s_1, a_3)$	$Q(s_1, a_4)$
s_2	$Q(s_2, a_1)$	$Q(s_2, a_2)$	$Q(s_2, a_3)$	$Q(s_2, a_4)$
s_3	$Q(s_3, a_1)$	$Q(s_3, a_2)$	$Q(s_3, a_3)$	$Q(s_3, a_4)$
s_4	$Q(s_4, a_1)$	$Q(s_4, a_2)$	$Q(s_4, a_3)$	$Q(s_4, a_4)$

Table 1: A sample 5x5 Q-table

Q-Learning, as a process, is how we iteratively change these Q-values such that after a certain number of repeated episodes, we can follow the intrinsic policy that is seen within it by continuously choosing the state-action pairs with the highest Q-values. The optimal policy that we are looking for is known as the **target policy**.

Initially, the agent doesn't know this target policy, so it starts essentially at random and the values in the Q-table is randomly loaded. This initial policy that will progressively get better is known as the **behavior policy**.

So, let's say that the agent takes a random action a from its initial state s_1 and transitions into state s_2. The way which we now quantify the value of that state-action pair is with an equation known as the **Bellman equation**, also known as the Bellman optimality equation.

Here is a simplified version of the Bellman equation for the above scenario:

$$Q(s_1, a) = R(s_2) + \gamma \arg \max_a (Q(s_2, a))$$

As you can see, the value of the last state-action pair is a function of the immediate reward and the best possible next state-action pair. Notice the discount factor γ which is applied to the next Q-value; this is done to prioritize current rewards over future rewards to encourage agents to obtain rewards as fast as possible without diminishing returns.

Great, we have updated the Q-value for the state-action pair that we just took. However, this value which we just calculated may not necessarily be in alignment with the Q-value which was already existing in the Q-table. This is due to the fact that the calculations took place at different time steps (remember time is discrete), so the relative value may have changed as a result of newly found information. This discrepancy between the newly calculated Q-value and the existing Q-value is known as a **Temporal Difference (TD) Error**.

We can write the TD error as the difference between the two:

$$TD = Q(s, a)_{new} - Q(s, a)_{old}$$

With this, we can take the TD error into account for our update of the Q-value:

$$Q(s, a)_{new} = Q(s, a)_{old} + \alpha(TD)$$

Notice the α symbol, which represents a parameter known as the **learning rate**, which is also called the step size. The learning rate determines how much the newly gathered information affects the older information. For purely deterministic problems, the α is typically set to 1, however, for stochastic problems, where information is typically convergent, a smaller value such as 0.1 is usually more efficient.

After accounting for the temporal difference error and adding the α parameter for controlling the flow of new information, the new Q-values are updated into the Q-table, which serve as a guide for the agent which gets more refined after each training episode.

Let's now introduce a side concept before we get started with more rigorously defining the Bellman optimality equation as you might see it in a lecture or a textbook. One of the primary balances that you need to strike when constructing a reinforcement learning algorithm is that between **exploration** and **exploitation**. Exploration can be defined a trying out new actions to discover their effects, and exploitation is using the knowledge which is already known (in our case, stored in the Q-table) and using that to maximize rewards.

You need to have both exploration and exploitation; if you only have exploration, you will learn a lot about the environment but never use your knowledge to obtain rewards. If you only have exploitation, sure, you may obtain rewards, but you may be separating yourself from decision pathways that provide greater rewards because you never explored them in the first place.

The way that we balance exploration and exploitation is with an ϵ-**greedy**, or epsilon greedy policy. The **hyperparameter** (a macro-scale parameter used to change model settings) ϵ refers to the probability of choosing to explore rather than exploit, and the greedy means that when exploiting, the highest state-action pair is chosen.

$$\begin{cases} P(\text{exploration}) = \epsilon \\ P(\text{exploitation}) = 1 - \epsilon \end{cases}$$

The above statement implies that $0 \leq \epsilon \leq 1$, which is true. The specific value of ϵ that is implemented, however, can vary. Do you want your Q-Learning model to be more ambitious but risk gaining rewards as a result? Do you want your model to be incredibly cautious, but have the possibility of being secluded into one particular state-action pathway whereas others could entail greater rewards? ϵ values should be updated accordingly based on personal needs and preferences.

From our previous discussions, you can probably infer that the ϵ value for Q-Learning tends towards the 0 than the 1; Q-Learning is deeply exploitation based, as it uses the Q-table as a explicit guide rather than a loose set of rules. Therefore, in most cases, Q-Learning ϵ-greedy policies will have $0.01 \leq \epsilon \leq 0.1$. Again, ϵ

is a subjective hyperparameter; it should be adjusted based on the needs and requirements of your agent and environment. However, those values are just what are most common in contemporary Q-Learning models.

One important thing to note when discussing ϵ-greedy policies are that they don't necessarily have to be static; the ϵ value can change throughout the course of the training process in order to be better suited towards the increasing amount of state-action information being obtained.

Typically, the ϵ values decay over training episodes, giving it the apt name of epsilon decay. This process is also known as epsilon annealing or simulated annealing.

When applying this to Q-Learning, epsilon decay can be particularly beneficial because you can start it very high in the beginning stages of training, which encourages exploration and thereby provides more information to the agent, and then end it with a very low value to capitalize on the knowledge which the agent should now be confident in.

Epsilon decay itself can be constructed in a multitude of ways, depending on the specifics of the agent and its environment. Typically, it is either linear or exponential in its decay factor; linear is kind of like a jack-of-all-trades, whereas exponential decay offers a smoother transition. The latter is particularly efficient if you want to prioritize exploration early on but then switch to exploration.

Linear decay can be broadly defined with a variety of different parameters. If ϵ_t represents the epsilon value at time t, its update as a function of its initial epsilon ϵ_0, minimum possible epsilon ϵ_{min}, and the total number of episodes n can be written as:

$$\epsilon_t = \epsilon_0 - \frac{t * (\epsilon_t - \epsilon_{min})}{n}$$

Exponential decay follows a similar pattern, except instead having a decay factor λ rather than a value n for the number of episodes. The formula looks reminiscent to a formula for something like continuous compounding in finance, only with decay instead of growth:

$$\epsilon_t = \epsilon_{min} + (\epsilon_0 - \epsilon_{min}) \times e^{\lambda t}$$

All things considered, you should be mindful of how you construct your ϵ-greedy policy with regards to the agent and the nature of the environment. If your optimal policy changes over time, linear decay may be better to maintain exploration for longer, and vice versa.

We'll come back to the concept of ϵ-greedy policies when we discuss implementing it in code, however, let's jump back into our discussion of the derivation of the traditional Q-Learning Bellman equation. Whereas our previous models and equations of it have been rather rudimentary and simplified, do let's now present the whole thing.

Now, some of this is going to be review, so just bare with me. However, there will be some new terminology and notation being introduced, so be sure to take note of that.

We'll start off with the Markov Decision Process (MDP), which we covered earlier. Just as a quick summary, we need to assume that our environment can be structured with the premise of an MDP, which implies that:

- There is a defined agent that is able to move throughout an environment, which can be defined in terms of conditional instances of it known as states. The agent's current state s must be within the set of all possible states, S; hence, $s \in S$.

- In order to transition between different states, the agent must take specific actions. The action that the agent is currently taking, a, must be in the set of all possible actions, A; $a \in A$.

- There must be a transition model, or transition function $P(s'|s, a)$ which adds stochasticity to the process. The action that an agent takes in a certain state isn't necessarily deterministic; it can lead to a multitude of outcomes. Therefore, this probabilistic function helps quantify that.

- Although each new state that the agent comes across doesn't necessarily have a reward, the reward function helps explain when it does. Typically represented as $R(s, a)$, the reward function simply defines the reward an agent receives after taking action a in state s.

- Finally, the last aspect of the MDP is the discount factor γ. The discount factor makes the agent short-sighted; it only cares about immediate rewards and places lesser value on future rewards. This has the inherent effect of preventing the agent from taking unnecessary actions and moving to unnecessary states. Thhe discount factor is a decay factor, so therefore $\gamma \in [0, 1]$.

The state-value function, which we are going to notate as $V^*(s)$, represents the maximum cumulative reward the agent can get when starting from initial state s, assuming optimal behavior. The Bellman Optimality Equation for the state-value function is expressed as a recursive function:

$$V^*(s) = \arg\max_a E_{s'}[R(s, a) + \gamma V^*(s')]$$

Now, this is definitely daunting, but let's compartmentalize it step-by-step:

- The $\arg\max$ operator at the beginning of the operation is kind of like a formality; it's basically just the mathematical way of saying in words "the agent will move optimally." However, if we are talking mathematically, the operator simply means that the agent must choose the action that leads to the next highest reward, kind of like a greedy algorithm.

- The $E_{s'}$ operation represents the expected value of the rewards in addition to all future values. The operation means that for all possible next states s', the expected value of that state and all future state is accumulated, assuming perfect agent performance action-wise.

- Finally, the multiplied term of $\gamma V^*(s')$ represents the discount factor being actively applied onto the future value function (which includes the future reward). This not only represents the recursive nature of this Bellman equation, which allows it to follow a path from beginning to end, but also show the priority for immediate rewards.

So, the overall idea is that the optimal value of the current state $V^*(s)$ is equal to the sum of the immediate reward and the discounted value of the next state, which needs to be done with the action that maximizes the sum.

The state-action value function (Q-function) takes on a similar Bellman formulation, however, let's quickly show the relationship between the state value function and the state-action value function. Quite simply:

$$V^*(s) = \arg\max_a Q^*(s, a)$$

The Q-function simply adds in the condition that the most optimal action will be chosen when in a particular state with multiple possible actions. The value of a state $V^*(s)$ and the state-action value function $Q(s, a)$ is that the former is the expected valuer of all Q-values weighted by their probabilities.

For essentially the same reasons as the state-value Bellman equation, the state-action Bellman equation or the Q-function can be written as:

$$Q^*(s, a) = E_{s'}[R(s, a) + \gamma \arg\max_a Q^*(s', a')]$$

In this case, the terms in this equation represent the following:

- $Q^*(s, a)$ represents the Q-value for being in the state s and taking action a, with the assumption that the agent will move optimally afterward. This is essentially just $V^*(s)$, just with the added parameter of action a.

- $R(s, a)$ is the same as in the state-value Bellman equation: the received reward as a result of taking action a in state s.

- The expression $\gamma \arg \max Q^*(s', a')$ represents the maximum future Q-value for the state s', given that the agent acts optimally and takes action a' from that state. Again, we are just adding an extra layer of complexity here with the optimal action parameter.

Ultimately, the state-action value function has the same elements as the state-value Bellman equation. However, this equation's goal is to find the expected cumulative reward from starting in state s, taking action a, the following the optimal policy from there by taking the maximum future Q-value, which has a discount factor γ applied to it to prioritize current rewards.

Now, let's try and move the state-action Bellman equation into the realm of Q-Learning, which is where we will reach the final form of the equation.

First of all, it is important to remember that Q-Learning is a **off-policy** algorithm, which means that it doesn't learn explicitly from a defined policy but rather uses greedy actions to construct what is essentially that policy. Therefore, Q-Learning doesn't require of the environment itself (i.e. the probability transition function $P(s'|s, a)$), but rather just sampled experiences of the parameters (s, a, r, s'), where:

- s: The current state
- a: The action taken in state s
- r: The reward received after taking action a
- s': The next state after action a

First, let's introduce the final equation we're going to tackle, the Q-Learning update rule, then show its derivation. The equation, in its most explicit form, is as follows:

$$Q(s, a) \mathrel{+}= \alpha[r + \gamma \arg\max_{a} Q(s', a') - Q(s, a)]$$

Now, a lot of the terms in this equation should look familiar, which is true because the majority of it is taken from the Bellman equations we just defined. Let's go step by step:

α is of course the learning rate ($\alpha \in [0, 1]$), which shows how much the new information overrides the old information. Typically, this value will be set at something like 0.1 for stochastic environments, so that the algorithm can converge more efficiently. However, in fully deterministic enviroments where there is no random chance, α can even be 1.

$r + \gamma \arg \max Q(s', a')$ should look familiar, as it is taken right from the state-action value Bellman equation we defined earlier. As you know, it is simply the sum of the current reward and the discounted future reward taken by going to the next state s'.

Why, however, does this sum have $Q(s, a)$ being subtracted from it? It all ties back to that concept of Temporal Difference (TD) errors which we mentioned earlier in the chapter. TD errors arise in reinforcement learning because the agent is making predictions (Q-values) about future rewards and outcomes, but these predictions are refined as new information is obtained by the agent.

In the case of Q-Learning, the gent doesn't know the exact total reward it'll receive by taking a particular action in a specific state. Instead, it predicts the Q-value ($Q(s, a)$), based on its past experiences and assumptions based on future events. These estimates, however, are often inaccurate or incomplete, especially early in the learning process where the agent hasn't learned very much information about the environment's intricacies.

Let's trace this back to the Q-Learning update rule. We know that $r + \gamma \arg\max_a Q(s', a')$ is the new information that the agent receives: it includes the the newly found reward. We typically refer to this value as the Temporal Difference (TD) Target. However, from this we must subtract the old information, which in this case is our old prediction about that state and the action we took to get there, or $Q(s, a)$. Therefore, from this, we can get the TD Error, which is:

$$\delta = r + \gamma \arg\max_a Q(s', a') - Q(s, a)$$

If we go back to a rudimentary equation which we defined earlier in this chapter

$$Q(s, a)_{new} = Q(s, a)_{old} + \alpha(TD)$$

we can realize that we are essentially just updating the new $Q(s, a)$ value by adding the magnitude of the change we want between timesteps as a function of the learning rate α. If the TD Error can be written as the δ defined above, we can therefore, conclude that the Q-Learning update rule is as follows:

$$Q(s, a) \mathrel{+}= \alpha[r + \gamma \arg\max_a Q(s', a') - Q(s, a)]$$

In this case, the $+=$ is just a shortened way of writing the update rule of $Q(s, a)_{new} = Q(s, a)_{old} +$ *some quantity*. We see that we are updating the TD Error δ by the learning rate α.

So, just to summarize:

We start out by defining the state-value Bellman optimality equation, which can be written as:

$$V^*(s) = \arg\max_a E_{s'}[R(s, a) + \gamma V^*(s')]$$

By using the following as a reference:

$$V^*(s) = \arg\max_a Q^*(s, a)$$

We can define a state-action value function, and use the same principles as before which estimates the expected cumulative reward when taking action a in state s and acting optimally thereafter:

$$Q^*(s, a) = E_{s'}[R(s, a) + \gamma \arg\max_a Q^*(s', a')]$$

By using the concept of TD Errors where the information that the agent possesses changes between different discrete time-steps, we can define a temporal difference error as follows:

$$\delta = r + \gamma \arg\max_a Q(s', a') - Q(s, a)$$

We can then account for this TD Error by multiplying it by a learning rate α, which can parameterize how much the robot takes into account new information in overriding previous information. Using this, we can update the Q-values in the Q-Learning update rule:

$$Q(s, a) \mathrel{+}= \alpha[r + \gamma \arg \max_a Q(s', a') - Q(s, a)]$$

And that's how we'll close out our discussion of the Q-Learning update rule and the Bellman equation. Now, when you first looked at them, they were probably very daunting, but now that we've taken it step by step, hopefully you realize that its construction is actually quite intuitive.

Let's get back to the idea of the Q-table, which is what actually gets updated by using this Q-Learning update rule. Just as a refresher, a Q-table looks something like this, with the number of possible states being the number of rows and the number of actions from these states being the number of columns. Here's a 4x4 Q-table:

Q	a_1	a_2	a_3	a_4
s_1	$Q(s_1, a_1)$	$Q(s_1, a_2)$	$Q(s_1, a_3)$	$Q(s_1, a_4)$
s_2	$Q(s_2, a_1)$	$Q(s_2, a_2)$	$Q(s_2, a_3)$	$Q(s_2, a_4)$
s_3	$Q(s_3, a_1)$	$Q(s_3, a_2)$	$Q(s_3, a_3)$	$Q(s_3, a_4)$
s_4	$Q(s_4, a_1)$	$Q(s_4, a_2)$	$Q(s_4, a_3)$	$Q(s_4, a_4)$

Let's discuss some of the limitations of the Q-table,

and why it may not be the most practical way of storing information in some reinforcement learning problems.

Let's start out with problems of **space complexity**, or the amount of physical data and memory that is required to store all of the Q-values. The Q-table requires a discrete and finite number of states and actions, so if the state-action space is too large or even continuous, using the Q-table effectively becomes impractical. For problems with many variables or continuous state-action spaces, the Q-table's complexity grows exponentially rather than linearly, which makes it much more computationally expensive and memory intensive.

For instance, a game like chess, which is not continuous but has an exceedingly large state-action space, is not something which can be easily modeled by a Q-table and therefore Q-Learning; there are other, more scalable methods of approximating state-action values other than Q-Learning.

Another big problem with the whole idea of the Q-table and Q-Learning in general is the lack of generalization. Q-Learning with a Q-table cannot generalize to unseen states, since every state-action pair must be explicitly seen and learned by the agent. Therefore, in order to get the most comprehensive Q-table, the agent essentially needs to visit every state-action combination in the environment to learn the optimal policy. In continuous or complex environments, this lack of generalization makes it so that the agent is unable to infer about nearby, similar states, making it less practical.

Now, this may make it sound like Q-Learning can't do anything, which is false. Q-Learning is a highly applicable technology, but there are things to do to improve its limitations (particularly those of the Q-table system).

The most common of these additions is something that we're actually going to cover in a lot more detail later in this book, which is known as **Deep Q-Learning**. Rather than using a linear approach with the Q-Learning update rule, Deep Q-Learning uses a neural network to approximate the Q-values, which not only makes predictions more accurate but also allows the agent to handle much large and continuous action spaces.

Another option is something called **state abstraction**. It's essentially just a way to reduce the dimensionality of the state space by using techniques that can group similar states together, which can reduce the size of the Q-table by grouping similar states together. This is reminiscent of unsupervised learning, where similar characteristics of various objects (in this case, states in the state-space) are grouped together in a process known as clustering.

One last option is called **hierarchical reinforcement learning**, which is a nuanced version of traditional reinforcement learning which can be used for more complex scenarios. Techniques like options and macro-actions, which can divide the state space into smaller, more manageable sub-problems that the agent can learn separately, can reduce the complexity of the Q-table.

Macro-actions essentially allow the agent to bypass the intermediate states that it may have to take and move to more distant states which therefore give a greater possibility of rewards. They can be uses to solve larger problems and speed up the learning process, improving performance on certain tasks.

Chapter 4:
GridWorld: Visualizing Q-Learning

Hopefully, you now have a deeper understanding of the underlying mathematical principles of not only Q-Learning, but also most of reinforcement learning. Admittedly, these concepts are very abstract and difficult to visualize, so let's use this chapter to break down the learning process in such a way that it becomes more comprehensible.

We'll start out by introducing an imaginary 2D enviroment known as GridWorld. As the name implies, its grid-like fashion will contain rewards (both positive and negative) for the agent to come across, and the ultimate idea is that the agent will be able to take an optimal path through this environment such that it is able to collect the most reward.

AGENT	-1	-1
-1	-1	-1
-1	-10	+10

Notice that we have -1 "reward" in all squares that aren't the large negative reward and large positive reward, which simply acts as a placeholder for the discount factor to prevent from actually having to compute that.

Remember, the ultimate goal of our agent is to reach that +10 square as effectively as possible. In other words, we want the agent to refine its target policy to reach +10 as efficiently as possible.

Now, remember that they way that Q-Learning makes decisions is by values stored in the Q-table. Just as a refresher, those values are stored in something like this:

Q	a_1	a_2	a_3	a_4
s_1	$Q(s_1, a_1)$	$Q(s_1, a_2)$	$Q(s_1, a_3)$	$Q(s_1, a_4)$
s_2	$Q(s_2, a_1)$	$Q(s_2, a_2)$	$Q(s_2, a_3)$	$Q(s_2, a_4)$
s_3	$Q(s_3, a_1)$	$Q(s_3, a_2)$	$Q(s_3, a_3)$	$Q(s_3, a_4)$
s_4	$Q(s_4, a_1)$	$Q(s_4, a_2)$	$Q(s_4, a_3)$	$Q(s_4, a_4)$

Table 2: Q-table

However, now that we are actually making decisions we need to initialize the Q-table with actual Q-values. As you may recall, these values are arbitrary to start out, but will eventually get honed as we proceed through more training cycles. However, we actually have a countable amount of actions and states that are in our 3x3 GridWorld example, so we can represent that with a Q-table.

The Q-table might look something like this:

Q	left	right	up	down
s_1	0.25	-1	0.33	0.75
s_2	0.9	0.4	0.3	-1.1
s_4	-1	0.7	1	0.4
...	...	...	...	...

Table 3: Arbitrary Q-table for 3x3 GridWorld

Now, let's say that as seen in the previous diagram, the agent starts in the upper-left corner in state s_1. The agent's initial decision, which can either be right or down, is dictated by the behavior policy, which is what handles all of the immediate decision making prior to converging onto the optimal policy.

Since the agent is acting randomly for the first training episode, let's assume that the agent goes downward. The agent then transitions into another state, which we can call s_4 if we order row-major.

Great, so we moved down to state s_4 and collected a -1 reward. So, let's update the Q-values accordingly. We can use a specific, simplified version of the Bellman equation to do so:

$$Q(s_1, \text{down})_{obs} = R(s_4) + \gamma \arg\max_a Q(s_4, a)$$

We know that the reward that we just got was -1, so we can plug that into the equation. For the next term, we can assume that the discount factor γ has a value of 0.9. As for the next possible highest Q-value, we need to refer back to the Q-table to obtain that information:

Q	left	right	up	down
s_1	0.25	-1	0.33	0.75
s_2	0.9	0.4	0.3	-1.1
s_4	-1	0.7	1	0.4
...	...	...	...	...

Table 4: Q-table for Bellman calculation

From the table, we can see that the maximum resultant Q-value after entering state s_4 is 1. From this, we can complete the equation by seeing that $-1 + 0.9 * 1 = -0.1$, so our observed Q-value for going down out of state s_1 is -0.1. However, we can see in the table above that $Q(s_1, \text{down})$ has a current value within the Q-table of 0.75, creating an aforementioned Temporal Difference (TD) error. Just to refresh, TD errors occur when Q-values are recalculated at different timesteps, and occur due to the onset of new information affecting the numerical value of the entry.

In our current example, the TD error can be represented as simply the differences between the observed and the expected Q-values:

$$\text{TD Error} = Q(s_1, \text{down})_{obs} - Q(s_1, \text{down})_{exp}$$

Therefore, in our example, the TD error can be calculated to be $-0.1 - 0.75 = -0.85$. We can now update the Q-value to its actual value by using a simplified Q-Learning update rule taking advantage of the TD error we just calculated as well as the learning rate α, which we can assume to be 0.25.

$$Q(s_1, \text{down}) \mathrel{+}= \alpha * \text{TD Error}$$

Therefore, our new $Q(s_1, \text{down})$ can be $0.75 + 0.25 * -0.85 = 0.5375$.

Now, this entire process is repeated over and over on multiple training episodes in order to keep refining these Q-values by first taking an action, calculating the observed Q-value and then the TD error, and finally using the Q-Learning update rule to get a final value to update in the Q-table.

Keep in mind, all of this is done within the framework of an ϵ-greedy policy, which means that we won't always necessarily choose the most ostensibly optimal state-action pair; we can choose to explore with a probability of ϵ which means we choose a sub-optimal state-action pair to start out. However, this may be a blessing in disguise, as this new state-action pair could lead to a better result than the current pathway we are stuck in now, so it's a gamble.

After we complete multiple of these training episodes, our Q-values are effectively "learned"; they will plateau and not change, which means that our training process is complete. However, after this, we can train the agent itself to follow the intrinsic policy which is found within the Q-table. By simply greedily taking the state-action pairs with the highest Q-value without any regard for an ϵ-greedy policy.

Typically, in the training process, you will run a Q-Learning model for a set number of training episodes then run that model using the greedy testing system to see how well it performs in collecting rewards. Usually, comparing the total collected rewards between overall training cycles can help inform environment-specific hyperparameter adjustments like ϵ, α, among others, as these are often hard to get correct first try.

Nevertheless, this quick visual introduction to Q-Learning as a process was should have proved insightful for you. We can now move on to programming and simulating Q-Learning with code, and seeing this learning process firsthand with actual reinforcement learning environments and agents. Please note that this was a very simplified example; in reality, the environment likely won't be such a small 2D environment but have various intricacies and depths within it. However, the same ideas should still apply, just to a more complex extent.

Chapter 5:
Coding Q-Learning with Python

Now that we have established the underlying mathematics of Q-Learning and visualized it, it is time to try coding Q-Learning and simulating the reinforcement learning process. For this, we will use Python, the most popular and readily accessible programming language for machine learning tasks.

We'll assume that you have a beginner to intermediate understanding of programming principles and the Python language, however, we will be going into detail of the finer details so that the bigger picture starts to take shape.

Let's start by importing the necessary libraries required for this program, which will contain the functions and software elements required for Q-Learning:

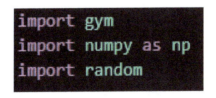

```
import gym
import numpy as np
import random
```

Figure 4: Python Libraries

Now, the first two libraries, numpy and random, should be familiar if you've done computational progammiing before. To introduce each of them:

- NumPy is a library for the Python language that is used to add support for more functional and multi-dimensional arrays, matrices, and other high-level mathematical operations. It is particularly well for storing data aggregates, and other tasks common in computer science and artificial intelligence like the dot and cross product for vectors.

- Random is the a Python library that does exactly what it says: take random noise and computer data and convert it into random numbers. Although computers can't theoretically simulate absolute randomness, the random library does its best with pseudo-random number generation.

The last library is what I want to draw attention to, however: `gymnasium` or `gym`.

The `gym` import is us loading in the reinforcement learning environment which our agent is going to be traversing through throughout it's many training episodes. This specific reinforcement learning environment is part of OpenAI's Gymnasium set of reinforcement learning environments. OpenAI created these environments for purposes like ours: allowing valuable testing for rudimentary and complex reinforcement learning models.

Although there are a lot of different environments to choose from in this library, for this example, we are going to use `FrozenLake-v1`, which can be imported with the following command: We have defined the `FrozenLake-v1` environment in a specific `environment` variable as a reference, which will be used throughout the rest of the program.

```
environment = gym.make("FrozenLake-v1", is_slippery = False)
```

Figure 5: Environment Initialization

Note that the `is_slippery` parameter included in this definition is OpenAI's way of including stochastic/deterministic processes in this reinforcement learning environment. If `is_slippery` is set to True, even if the agent decides to take one of the four actions (up, right, left, down), the agent has a chance of slipping and going in an unintended direction.

Therefore, `is_slippery` can be used if you want a more robust policy that can navigate uncertainties at the expense of a more intensive training volume.

Now that the initialization and loading processes are out of the way, it's now time to start building our Q-Learning model. The first thing we have to do is define values called hyperparameters, which are parameters that define the learning process. Hyperparameters include the learning rate α, the discount factor γ, the epsilon value ϵ for the ϵ-greedy policy, and finally, the number of training episodes. These can be defined as follows:

```
learning_rate = 0.1
epsilon = 0.1
decay_factor = 0.99
num_episodes = 2000
```

Figure 6: Environment Initialization

Although previously we have visualized the Q-table as vestigial to the learning process, we need to explicitly define it in our program. For this, we can use the `np.zeros()` function to define a table of zeros, and use parameters inherent to the environment to define its size. `environment.observation_space.n` can be used to define all possible states, and likewise `environment.action_space.n` can be used to define all possible actions.

```
Q = np.zeros((environment.observation_space.n, environment.action_space.n))
```

Figure 7: Environment Initialization

Okay, now that all of the pre-training preparation is done, we can start simulating episodic training. To start, we can construct a for-loop iterating `num episodes` times, and reset the current state using `environment.reset()`. The `done` variable represents having moved to the next state, which will be turned `True` when completed. For now, we'll create a while-loop to proceed with the training process until we reach the next state, after which we'll break out of it.

Okay, the next step is to implement the ϵ-greedy policy. Although I detailed a lot of fancy versions of this exploration system like linear and exponential decay, for now, we're just going to use a constant ϵ value.

```python
if random.uniform(0, 1) < epsilon:
    action = environment.action_space.sample()
else:
    action = np.argmax(Q[state])
```

Figure 8: Epsilon-Greedy Policy

In the above image, we construct a conditional to represent the ϵ-greedy policy. As you know, it can be mathematically defined as:

$$\begin{cases} P(\text{exploration}) = \epsilon \\ P(\text{exploitation}) = 1 - \epsilon \end{cases}$$

The way we choose the epsilon value is by using the `random` library. Using the `random.uniform()` command, we can generate a random number between the selected lower and upper bound (0 and 1), and use that as a comparison for our ϵ value.

Okay, let's now look at what we do each step of the way. With a probability of ϵ, we are supposed to choose the "exploration" pathway. In code, we do this by sampling a new state from the current possible action-space; this can be done with the command `environment.actionspace.sample()`. With a probability of $1 - \epsilon$ we choose the "exploitation pathway," meaning we choose the best possible numerical action based on the current state.

In Python, we can do so by using a numerical function from NumPy: `np.argmax()`, which simply chooses/returns the highest value based on the input parameter. In this case, `np.argmax(Q[state])` chooses the index of the action with the highest Q-value in the Q-table; in other words, it selects from the domain, not the range.

Okay, that is the ϵ-greedy policy implemented in our Python code. Once we've made this decision on whether or not to pursue exploration or exploitation, we actually need to move the agent to the next state and receive any possible rewards.

We can do so with the following bit of code:

```
next_state, reward, done, _ = environment.step(action)
```

Figure 9: Step-Function for taking actions

We can use the `environment.step(action)`

command to execute the agent going to the next state based on the action we decided from the ϵ-greedy policy. Notice that the `environment.step()` function returns a few different values:

- `nextstate`: Pretty self explanatory here, just return the variable instance of the next state that the agent entered as a result of taking the previous action

- `reward`: The immediate reward that was collected by the agent. Notice how later on the reward isn't tallied or totaled, but merely collected. If we wanted to see the reward ourselves, we could add a print statement with a continuously incrementing amount whenever we receive a reward.

- `done`: This goes back to the done variable that we created outside of the for-loop; this done variable will only be turned true when we reach a terminal state. For our first pass through the training process, we can assume that the done variable is still `False`.

- That last parameter is seen as empty; don't worry about it for now, the `environment.step()` function technically returns four parameters, but we only need the first three, so we place an underscore as a placeholder to fill in for that value which we aren't going to use in this simple demonstration.

We have now moved the agent to the next state and received any applicable rewards; time to update the Q-table with our findings. We do this with the following one-liner representing a Python version of the Q-Learning update rule:

```
Q[state, action] = Q[state, action] + learning_rate * [reward + decay_factor * np.max(Q[next_state]) - Q[state, action]]
```

Figure 10: Epsilon-Greedy Policy

Now, this should look extremely similar to the mathematical Q-Learning update rule:

$$Q(s, a) \mathrel{+}= \alpha[r + \gamma \arg\max_{a} Q(s', a') - Q(s, a)]$$

However, just in case there are some doubts to clear out, here is a quick summary of the terms:

- Q[state, action] is just the code way of referencing $Q(s, a)$; typically for two-dimensional arrays, square brackets are used to signify array indices.

- np.max(Q[nextstate]) is mathematically how $\arg\max Q(s', a')$ is done. Remember, np.argmax() and np.max() are two different things; in our case, we are inputting the next state as an input into the Q-function and looking for the highest action, not the index of the highest action as we did with the ϵ-greedy policy.

70

Finally, we must of course move to the next state which we reached by using the `environment.step()` command by setting the previous variable equal to the new value. This is seen in code here:

```
state = next_state
```

Figure 11: State-Switching

That concludes the code implementation training-wise. Hopefully the steps we're pretty intuitive, as its essentially just following steps and concepts that you've learned in previous concepts and putting it all together to simulate the process with a real programming language.

We start out in a randomized state using the function `environment.reset()`, and initialize the 2-D Q-table by using the function `np.zeros()`. We assign our hyperparameters to variables, then continuously loop the training process until we reach a terminal state by using an `done` variable.

To implement the ϵ-greedy policy, we can use the `random.uniform()` function to simulate the probabilistic outcome, then either sample an new action or use `np.argmax()` to simulate choosing the most valuable action.

We then use `environment.step()` to actually move the agent to the next state and receive any rewards, and use a coded version of the Q-Learning update rule to use that information to change Q-values. We then change to the next state and repeat the process.

After we train the model, we can test it by just continuously using `np.argmax()` on state-action pairs to follow the intrinsic policy, which can be done with the following code:

```
state = environment.reset()
environment.render()

while not done:
    action = np.argmax(Q[state])
    state, reward, done, _ = environment.step(action)
    environment.render()

print(f"Reward: {reward}")
```

Figure 12: State-Switching

You'll notice the `environment.render()` commands included throughout the testing process, which simply adds a GUI to the screen which allows you to visualize the movements and collection of rewards by the agent, which makes the process more comprehensible. This is not absolutely necessary, but just something nice to have.

Chapter 6:
Applications and Improvements to Q-Learning

We touched on a couple of the drawbacks of Q-Learning in previous chapters, so now we can delve into their solutions and additions to Q-Learning that we can add on top of the original algorithm. We mentioned a couple of them before, but now I really want to explain their intricacies and details, similar to how the details of the Bellman equation were explained in in Chapter 3.

Let's start off with a very popular extension of the Q-Learning algorithm, which is known as Deep Q-Learning. Deep Q-Learning is designed to handle environments with large state-action spaces, which is a problem when using traditional Q-Learning due to logical and space constraints with the Q-table.

Just to refresh, Q-Learning wants to define a function $Q(s, a)$ that can estimate expected future rewards based on the current state s in which action a is taken and then the optimal policy is followed afterward. This is represented recursively by the state-action Bellman equation:

$$Q^*(s, a) = E_{s'}[R(s, a) + \gamma \arg \max_a Q^*(s', a')]$$

We can then episodically update the values in a Q-table by using the following update rule for Q-values:

$$Q(s, a) \mathrel{+}= \alpha[r + \gamma \arg\max_{a} Q(s', a') - Q(s, a)]$$

Now, as we know, it is impractical to store all of the $Q(s, a)$ values in a tabular structure, so Deep Q-Learning instead uses a neural network to approximate the Q-function itself.

Let's introduce some new notation to understand this better. As you know, neural networks contain individual computational units known as neurons in them, which when working in coordination, can be use to store and process large amounts of information. Neurons themselves are made up of two parameters, weights which linearly multiply input data based on its magnitude, and biases which can provide further scaling within multiplying the input data.

We can use these quantitative parameters to our advantage to store data, particularly the weights since they hold greater importance in the overall scaling/shifting of data. We can represents the weights of the neural network that we are using for Deep Q-Learning with θ. This idea behind this Q-network overall is that we are to input the current state s into the network, and get an output vector of Q-values for every possible action a in that state.

Just like in traditional Q-Learning, the aim of deep Q-

Learning is to train the neural network to be able to minimize the difference between the expected Q-value and the Q-value which is predicted by the network. Also, just like in Q-Learning, the expected Q-value contains two parts, which are derived from the Bellman equation:

- The immediate reward r, or $R(s, a)$. This is the reward which is immediately given to the agent upon entering a favorable state which positively affects the changes in Q-values.

- The discounted maximum Q-value of the next state, $\gamma \arg \max Q^*(s', a', \theta^-)$. Notice how an extra parameter, θ^-, was added, which in this case represents the weights and biases of the target network. In Deep Q-Learning, there are two networks, the main Q-network and the target network. The Q-network is the network that is actively being updated and changed, which approximates the Q-function $Q(s, a, \theta)$. The target network is another network which works in tandem with the Q-network; although the weights and biases of the Q-network are volatile, the target network serves as a reference, as its weights and biases, θ^-, are only updated sparingly. Typically, a hyperparameter N is included in Q-Learning to show how many timesteps it should take before updating the target network.

Just like in Q-Learning, Deep Q-Learning can have

Temporal Difference (TD) errors that result from the agent gaining new information between timesteps that is not represented in the Q-values themselves. The TD error in this case, however, can also show the difference between the target network and the Q-network, which we are similarily trying to converge. With this in mind, the temporal difference error in Deep Q-Learning can be represented as:

$$\delta = r + \delta \arg\max_a Q(s', a', \theta^-) - Q(s, a, \theta)$$

For neural networks in general, the primary aim is to minimize the loss function, which fundamentally represents the difference between the model predictions and the real data. In the case of Deep Q-Learning, we can used TD error to construct our loss function. However, we have to square the TD error for a couple of reasons:

- Least-square approaches are common in machine learning which require a square of the error function; the squared TD error δ^2 can be used to measure how far the network's current Q-value is from the target Q-value.

- In addition, the smoother, quadratic nature of δ^2 provides for a smooth, convex loss function that is better for optimization algorithms like gradient descent, which are used to progressively decrease the network's loss.

So, with this idea of δ^2 error being representative of our loss function, we can write the following as the explicit version of such:

$$L(\theta) = E[\delta^2]$$
$$\delta = r + \delta \arg\max_a Q(s', a', \theta^-) - Q(s, a, \theta)$$

Okay, now we have defined a loss function for our Q-Learning neural networks. Let's get into the actual learning and training process of how these networks actually make decisions and improve the performance of our agent.

In Q-Learning, the experiences of the agent in each episode are sort of encoded into the Q-values within an Q-table, which can make it a bit hard for the agent to make informed decisions about which states to try and reach/avoid and what corresponding actions the agent should take.

Deep Q-Learning avoids this by storing experiences of the agent explicitly in something called the experience replay buffer, which we can represent with D. The experience buffer stores the same information as does the sampled experiences in regular Q-Learning:

- s: The current state
- a: The action taken in state s

- r: The reward received after taking action a

- s': The next state after action a

During the training itself, the agent samples mini-batches of transitions from $D(s, a, r, s')$, and the loss function is compured accordingly. The way that the weights are updated of the Q-network can be summarized in the following equation:

$$\theta \leftarrow \theta - \eta \nabla_\theta L(\theta)$$

Let's break this down step-by-step:

- θ, as we know, represents the weights and biases of the Q-network, which is the network that we are doing the majority of our updates on.

- η is the learning rate, so to speak, for the neural network training process. Similar to the α parameter in the Q-Learning update, rule, η can show how much the gradient descent of the loss function affects the policy

- $\nabla_\theta L(\theta)$ represents the gradient for the loss with respect to the network's weights and biases, θ. This is very similar to gradient descent and backpropagation in traditional neural networks, where we are slowly updating our networks weights and biases in the direction that minimizes the loss function, which is a broad function that represents the network's performance.

So, sampled experienced of $D(s, a, r, s')$ are taken from the agent and environment, piped into the loss function with the parameter of the Q-network's weights and biases θ, then updated accordingly by using η as a parameter to control the flow of new information affecting the old.

Deep Q-Learning also implements ϵ-greedy policies as does regular Q-Learning. Just to refresh, ϵ-greedy policies have a balance between exploration and exploitation where they balance random actions from following the optimal policy. This can be summarized probabilistically as:

$$\begin{cases} P(\text{exploration}) = \epsilon \\ P(\text{exploitation}) = 1 - \epsilon \end{cases}$$

where ϵ is a hyperparamater that can be changed and defined as needed.

Before we transition into some other concepts, I want to quickly detail some of the historical uses of Deep Q-Learning, so you can better get an understanding for the type of problems its does well in.

Arguably the most popular use of Deep Q-Learning was with Google's DeepMind program that underwent research from around 2013 to 2015. The use of Deep Q-Learning was simple: teach it to play simple pixelated Atari 2600 games, which it was able to do successfully. This constituted a major breakthrough in reinforcement learning: the fact that the Deep Q-Learning algorithm was able to learn effective policies (game strategies) from such high-dimensional input spaces (images), without any knowledge of the game's rules or mechanics makes it truly a marvel of AI.

It was best applied in games like Breakout and Space Invaders; the agent in these networks was able to supercede human performance in these games. The input in these games was of course the raw color and pixel data from the screen itself, and the output was a Q-value for each possible action (left, right, shooting, etc.).

Programming high-performance Atari games using Q-Learning would have proved almost impossible: the extremely large state-space due to the dynamic image input and the stochasticity of the scenarios led to the need for more advanced algorithms, which is what saw the growth of Deep Q-Learning, which essentially stemmed out of and became popular as a result of this research by DeepMind.

DeepMind has done lots of other exciting work. After the huge success of their Atari game automation with Deep Q-Learning, they began developing an agent to play the ancient board game of Go. Named

AlphaGo, the model uses a variety of different under-lying computer science and mathematical techniques, like Monte Carlo Tree Search and deep neural net-works, it used Deep Q-Learning early on in its training cycle that led to its eventual growth in computational power.

AlphaGo initially used Q-Learning and other rein-forcement learning algorithms to make its decisions; however, in later stages, these technologies were added onto in order to make search mechanism and decision making more efficient.

Briefly, we can go over a couple more broad use cases of Deep Q-Learning outside of the incredible work that was done and is still being done by the DeepMind team:

- Deep Q-Learning has been used in robotics and autonomous control; it can be use for robotic arm manipulation, where task-specific objectives like grasping an object or reaching a target location work as rewards. States as captured by the sensors on the arm, and actions are represented by dif-ferent combinations of motor commands. It has also been used in fields like autonomous driving, where states are determined by the sensors on the car (cameras, LIDAR, etc.), actions are decisions like steering, accelerating, and breaking, and rewards are related to good driving practices like staying in lanes and avoiding collisions.

- Healthcare has also seen the integration of Deep Q-Learning. Its uses include interpreting patient data in order to come up with treatment options, where the reward function is based on past patient outcomes, which can be used to improve the model's health metrics for increased accuracy.

Okay, that about wraps up our discussion of Deep Q-networks and Deep Q-Learning, which is the most important addition on top of traditional Q-Learning. In a second, you'll see rapid descriptions of a couple of other Q-Learning improvements, which you can feel free to research if you are interested in learning more about them.

One common example of something building off of traditional Q-Learning is the seemingly next best thing: Double Q-Learning. Although it sounds simple, it can actually be used to mitigate some of the major flaws that are seen with traditional Q-Learning without bringing in an advanced structure like a neural network to counteract it.

Double Q-Learning is an improvement over traditional Q-Learning which is designed to remove bias from the latter, specifically overestimation bias. You see, in standard Q-Learning, the agent uses the same

Q-values for selecting the best action (the intrinsic policy) and estimating the value of that action itself (Q-Learning update rule). Therefore, it's kind of like a double-counting error, where the same high value is being used for two tasks at once, which may lead to over-optimistic value estimates in particularly complex or noisy environments.

The Q-Learning update rule is as follows:

$$Q(s, a) \mathrel{+}= \alpha[r + \gamma \arg\max_a Q(s', a') - Q(s, a)]$$

The important thing to note is that the action selection, $\arg\max Q(s', a')$ and the action evaluation $Q(s', a')$ are both based on the same Q-function. Therefore, the double use of these Q-values can cause overestimation, since the $\arg\max$ operator selects higher values even if some are overly optimistic due to random fluctuations and noise.

Double Q-Learning mitigates this by breaking down the action selection and evaluation into two different Q-functions. These functions, Q_A and Q_B, should be used and updated independently to mitigate any overestimation.

The way that updates are split between the two functions is simply by using probability. During each update, one of the two Q-functions is randomly chosen to be the action function (which selects the best action via $\arg\max$), and the other is used to evaluate it, which breaks the correlation between action selection and function evaluation.

The update-rule for Double Q-Learning, therefore, becomes a lot more complex. It now requires two possible equations, each with an equal likelihood of occurring and either choosing Q_A or Q_B.

With a probability of 0.5, we can update $Q_A(s, a)$ with the following on the right side of the update rule:

$$\alpha[r + \gamma Q_B(s', \arg\max_a Q_A(s', a')) - Q_A(s, a)]$$

Similarly, with a probability of 0.5, we can update $Q_B(s, a)$ on the right side of that update rule:

$$\alpha[r + \gamma Q_A(s', \arg\max_a Q_B(s', a')) - Q_B(s, a)]$$

Okay, that's the basic premise of Double Q-Learning, which is just building off of traditional Q-Learning and the Q-Learning update rule in order to reduce overestimation bias as mentioned before. Aside from just reducing that, however, Double Q-Learning also has some other benefits that go along with the probabilistic update model:

- Double Q-Learning itself gives more accurate value estimates, as the alternation between the two Q-functions leads to more accurate evaluation of policies, which therefore leads to better policies in general particularly in stochastic and noisy environments.

- As you may have already assumed, Double Q-Learning converges faster, due to the lesser overestimation leading to more reliable predictions and evaluations of the dual-update rule setup.

Let me give an example agent-environment setup where double Q-Learning would be more beneficial that traditional Q-Learning. Just like we've simulated before, there is an agent in a grid-world setup, where certain actions or strings of actions give stochastic rewards. With a standard Q-Learning model, the agent is likely to go around the grid-world and overestimate the value of certain actions, because the randomness (stochasticity) of the rewards makes those actions appear better than they actually are. However, if the agent was to instead use Double Q-Learning, the two Q-functions working in parallel would be less likely to overestimate, because one function selects the action and the other evaluates it based on its own, independently updated values.

For these reasons, Double Q-Learning has been seen as a positive addition on top of the traditional Q-

Learning schematic. Although it does still run into similar problems with space constraints of the Q-table, Double Q-Learning has been used extensively in fields such as reinforcement learning, particularly in noisy and unpredictable environments. Therefore, it's most common uses are in dynamic problems like robotics and autonomous control, resource management, etc.

We already learned that ϵ-greedy policies are one of the ways for a Q-Learning model to balance exploitation and exploration in its episodic learning process. However, let's introduce you to another, more complex strategy of doing so, which is known as Boltzmann exploration. Similar to ϵ-greedy policies, the Boltzmann exploration system balances exploiting new information in an intrinsic policy and exploration of new actions that could potentially lead to higher rewards.

The foundation of Boltzmann exploration is the Boltzmann distribution, which uses the softmax function to convert Q-values into probabilities. Mathematically, the softmax function is used to transform a vector of real numbers into a probability distribution, where each value in the vector is mapped to a probability between 0 and 1. The softmax function can be constructed as follows:

Let's assume we have a vector of real numbers $z = \langle z_1, z_2, z_3, ..., z_n \rangle$ from which we want to produce the probability distribution $p = \langle p_1, p_2, p_3, ..., p_n \rangle$. We can compute each probability p_i as the following:

$$p_i = \frac{e^{z_i}}{\sum_{j=1}^{n} e^{z_j}}$$

The exponential function is used to guarantee a positive number and to accentuate the differences between the values, and we divide by the sum of all the exponentiated values at the end to normalize the distribution, just as we do when calculating the mean of an integer dataset.

For the case of Boltzmann exploration in Q-Learning, we replace the vector z with the Q-function $Q(s, a)$. The agent chooses an action a with a probability of $P(a)$ by applying the softmax function to the Q-values for all available actions in the current state s.

This can be represented with the following:

$$P(a) = \frac{e^{Q(s,a)/\tau}}{\sum_{a'} e^{Q(s,a')/\tau}}$$

You should have noticed the τ hyperparameter that was added into the Boltzmann exploration softmax function. This parameter is known as temperature, and can be used to control how much exploration that the agent performs. Let's walk through each of the possibilities:

- When the temperature τ is high, the probability distribution becomes more uniform, which means that the agent will choose to explore more, since the probabilities dictate the change of choosing a new action. The higher that the τ value is, the less emphasis that is placed on the Q-values, and therefore, action selection is almost entirely random.

- As the temperature τ decreases, however, the agent becomes more greedy and less explorative. Lower τ values make the agent more likely to select actions with higher Q-vales, reducing exploration and focusing on exploiting the best-known actions. If you didn't realize, the τ parameter from Boltzmann exploration and the ϵ parameter from ϵ-greedy policies have an inverse relationship.

- When the τ parameter become 0, the agent is performing a direct greedy policy, where the highest Q-value action is taken all the time, which can lead to being stuck in a path of lower rewards throughout the entire episodic learning process.

Now, just like with ϵ-greedy policies, the hyperparameter τ itself doesn't always have to remain the same; it can decay or grow as needed. However, if you do choose to keep τ constant, it can be somewhat challenging to pick an exact value, as it is relatively problem-specific.

Okay, let's discuss one more addition on top of Q-Learning, which is known as Hierarchical Q-Learning, which we touched on in a previous chapter.

Hierarchical Q-Learning, as a concept, is simply an extension of traditional Q-Learning where the complex tasks and problems native to it are broken down into smaller, simpler subtasks. This is achieved by structuring the problem itself into smaller, more manageable subtasks, then using that framework to handle decision making.

Let's look at some of the key concepts of Hierarchical Q-Learning:
First off, in Hierarchical Q-Learning, tasks themselves are decomposed into smaller and more manageable pieces. This is done by having agent(s) not only learn how to act in the environment but also how to structure and sequence subtasks to achieve long-term goals:

- The primary task is divided into smaller subtasks which are called options or macro-actions
- Each option is treated as if its a smaller Q-Learning problem, where the goal is to learn to solve that smaller problem as optimally as possible
- The higher-level agent decides which subtask to

execture, while lower-level agents solve these sub-tasks

Also, typically within hierarchical Q-Learning, there are also two (or even more) sets of policies themselves, which can make decisions either at the macro or micro level:

- The higher-level policy selects an option or sub-task to solve based on the current state, and maintains a higher-level Q-function which spans over all of the possible options. This policy is a macro-policy which handles the structure and order of the options themselves, whereas

- The lower-level policy handles the work within each sub-task or option, where these policies handle traditional Q-Learning setups to achieve goals that are set by the higher-level policy. The lower-level policy is essentially controlled by the higher-level policy, and the lower-level policy directly controls the agent's work in performing these lower tasks. The higher-level policy indirects affects the agent by giving it a rough framework, which is then detailed by the lower-level policy.

One last thing to consider with this idea of Hierarchical Q-Learning is the idea of time abstraction and extension. Although we've traditionally looked at the Q-Learning decision making process as being confined to a single time step, Hierarchical Q-Learning allows for the policy to select options that may extend over a couple of even many time steps. This is part of the aforementioned long-term planning which is controlled by the higher-level policy and implemented by the lower-level policy.

Okay, those are the most common concepts when it comes to additions onto Q-Learning itself, which were presented with some real-world use cases of each. In the next chapter, we'll discuss the code implementations for each of these concepts, and wrap up our discussion of Q-Learning and transition to related topics like model-based reinforcement learning.

Chapter 7:
A Snapshot of On-Policy Reinforcement Learning

The content of this chapter isn't entirely related to Q-Learning, but rather a continuation of our broader discussion of reinforcement learning. As you know, there are two broad categories to reinforcement learning algorithms: value-based reinforcement learning (including Q-Learning) and policy-based (on-policy) reinforcement learning. Value-based reinforcement learning uses an intrinsic policy to guide its agent, whereas policy-based reinforcement learning explicitly tweaks the parameters of the policy itself.

But, to start off, why? Why do we need policy-based reinforcement learning if value-based reinforcement learning seems just as good, especially when all of the additions and tweaks are added to the various algorithms/systems within it. Well, instead of fixing the inherently flawed algorithm that is Q-Learning, why not just start from scratch and make something to mitigate those issues entirely. That's what machine learning engineers were thinking when they designed policy-based reinforcement learning, a relatively contemporary development.

Policy-based reinforcement learning, in theory, should be able to mitigate lots of the problems that are seen with value-based methods. It is able to handle continuous and high-dimensional action spaces; not having the intermediate computational step of using the Q-values but instead directly updating the policy makes this method a lot more efficient.

Furthermore, value-based methods are weak with stochastic environments; in fact, they're almost entirely only useful in deterministic environments or those in between. However, the direct influencing of the agent's policy instead of indirectly influencing it makes it more inclined to simulate stochastic behavior, which is why it becomes more beneficial in those use cases, which are more common. Again, having stochastic policies aren't necessary, but it makes the agent's handling of problems much more robust.

In policy-based reinforcement learning, the goal is to develop an explicit policy $\pi(a|s)$ that can map the connections between states and actions, and decide the next action based on the current state.

The end goal behind policy-based reinforcement learning is ultimately the same, however: obtain the maximum cumulative reward over episodic training intervals. In Q-Learning, this is done by using the Q-Learning update rule to prioritize current rewards rather than later rewards, but this principle doesn't necessarily apply to policy-based reinforcement learning, where the reward calculations are done more definitively.

So, how do we directly interact with the policy π in order to make tangible decisions between state-action transitions? Let's start off with some new (and some old) information about policy-based reinforcement learning:

- Just like with value-based reinforcemnt learning, we should assume that the problem statement falls within the grounds of a Markov Decision Process. This also assumes that $s \in S, a \in A$, and γ exist, and that the functions $P(s'|s, a)$ and $R(s, a)$ are well-defined.

- Policy-based reinforcement learning methods are typically stochastic, so that means that actions don't have definitive consequences.

- The end goal of policy-based reinforcement learning is to optimize a function $J(\theta)$, where J is the expected reward under the θ parameters of the policy.

Let's dig deeper into the $J(\theta)$ function, which we can simply call the objective function. The return of this function is the sum of rewards over a set period of time. Naturally, we want to maximize this function.

Unlike the loss function in neural networks, which we want to minimize and therefore use gradient descent for, this function uses the exact opposite: gradient ascent. Therefore we find the gradient of the function at a specific, parameterized point, and then use that to step in the positive direction towards a "peak."

Rather than working quantitatively by continuously taking the highest state-action Q-value, the policy directly creates a series of steps, known as a trajectory. Typically this trajectory is represented by τ, and follows a chronological progression similar to $\langle s_0, a_0, s_1, a_1, ... \rangle$

Okay, now that we have discussed the objective function, let's get into the specifics of how the gradient ascent function works.

The function itself can be defined as:

$$\nabla_\theta J(\theta) = E[\nabla_\theta \log \pi_\theta(a|s) Q^\pi(s, a)]$$

The specifics of how the algorithm works won't be provided, but here is the gist:

- The $Q^\pi(s, a)$ is the action-value function, which represents the maximum cumulative reward from state s, taking action a, and following policy π afterward.

- $\log \pi_\theta$ represents the log-probability of taking action a under policy π_θ. To put it simply, the log probability drastically reduces the computational complexity of the probabilities within the policy, which is what allows it to handle complex action spaces and stochastic policies.

We are, therefore, analyzing the gradient of the expected return with respect to the policy parameters θ and adjusting them in the direction of the higher reward.

The most prevalent policy-based reinforcement learning algorithm is known as Proximal Policy Optimization (PPO), which combines the stability and performance of policy-based reinforcement learning methods.

If we take the policy parameters to be θ, we can assume that a traditional policy update method would look something like this:

$$\theta_{new} = \theta_{old} + \alpha * \nabla_\theta J(\pi_\theta)$$

This linear update uses a learning-rate system represented by α, and we simply step in the positive direction of the gradient under parameters θ and under policy π_θ.

However, one of the big problems with regular policy gradient methods is that large policy changes can lead to instability. If the policy shifts too much, actions might be taken that are significantly worse than before. Although its hypothetical, imagine if the current policy is doing well and picking actions with higher probabilities, but then after one big update, it starts picking worse and worse actions which are not recoverable from. This severely hinders the learning process; we need a system that's able to resist negative actions more effectively as so that we don't get stuck in a negative action rabbit hole.

The way that PPO mitigates this is by constructing a clipping mechanism that is able to ensure that the new policy doesn't significantly deviate from the old policy. This is done through the construction of a ratio comparing the two, namely the importance sampling ratio.

The ratio, $r(\theta)$ can be written as:

$$r(\theta) = \frac{\pi_\theta(a|s)}{\pi_{\theta_{old}}(a|s)}$$

where the numerator is the new policy after a policy update and the denominator is the old policy prior to the policy update. The value of the importance sampling ratio is what is valuable to the decision making process with PPO.

Logically, we can assume the following with this ratio:

- If $r(\theta) < 1$, the new policy is less likely to take a particular action than the old policy; the new policy is more conservative with its decisions.

- If $r(\theta) > 1$, the new policy is more likely to take a particular decision that the old policy; the new policy is more liberal with its decision making.

- In the rate case that $r(\theta) = 1$, the two policies are equally likely to make a decision; the two are essentially parametrically equal.

The ultimate objective behind this clipping process is to of course maximize the expected reward, but also prevent the importance sampling ratio from becoming too small or too large (keep it stable at around 1). If we were to deviate too far, that may indicate a drastic change in the policy, which is generally unfavorable, as mentioned earlier. One bad step which significantly changes the policy may be difficult to recover from if not acted on quickly. This can be detrimental, so the ratio is a safeguard of sorts; it doesn't prevent the negative actions themselves from happening, but it lessens their impact on the agent's behavior within the environment as a whole.

This ratio will be referred to variably, but just know that it represents the essentially the difference before and after a policy update, with the magnitude representing how drastic of a shift that update was from the norm.

PPO also runs on something similar, but not a copy of the Q-function which is known as the advantage function, which we will be referring to as A. The advantage function, quite simply, just tells you how good or bad an action was, similar to how Q-values denote how good a state-action pair is within an agent's intrinsic policy. This A function will be used later.

The models we've been using in the past have a lot of hyperparameters, or parameters that control the settings within the model and indirectly influencing the agent rather than directly influencing them. In our case, we will use β to represent the maximum range which we don't want $r(\theta)$ to exceed.

Chapter 8: Conclusion

Well, you made it! Congratulations for making it this far in the book and gaining a solid understanding of reinforcement learning, Q-Learning, and the various related algorithms that go along with it. From the bottom of my heart, I, the author, would like to thank you for choosing this book to introduce you to such a valuable topic; it does mean a lot to me as this is my first book!

Now, you would have learned a lot of different concepts if you read this book all the way through, so I want to just give you some other topics which you may find interesting to learn about as a supplement to what you've already learned.

You've seen enough diagrams and equations by now, so I won't at all go into much detail about each of these algorithms. Instead, I'll simply introduce them and hope that in the future, you'll choose to research them, as I've found that they all logically relate back to the ideas of artificial intelligence, machine learning, and the topic of this book, Q-Learning. These concepts can either clarify what you've learned in this book or add new algorithms and systems to your growing toolbox.

One of the biggest focuses that I had when writing this book was bringing everything down to its fundamental steps: how does this work and why does it work? The main way I've done that is by simply showing the equations relevant to reinforcement learning and done any relevant derivations, so the entire process is clear about the algorithm itself.

One algorithm that I didn't touch on in too much detail but frequently referred to was the idea of back-propagation. As you should know, back-propagation is what neural networks use to progressively train and update their weights and biases. This process in general can be extrapolated to a lot of different concepts, including those we covered in this book. For example, the episodic tweaking of the Q-values stored in the Q-table is reminiscent of the honing of weights and biases in the neural network. Just for clarity, in neural networks, training episodes are instead referred to as training epochs.

For anyone remotely interested in deep learning, or the study of neural networks as it relates to artificial intelligence, I would highly recommend getting a fundamental understanding of the mathematical and programming principles behind not only traditional neural networks but specialized ones as well.

I will warn you, back-propagation is not a very easy concept; it's very conceptual and math-heavy. However, some of the concepts we've used here are applied and could be useful for your understanding. For instance, gradient descent is applied in back-propagation and the overall training process. If you have a background in multivariable calculus, the entire process will be much more comprehensible; since there are so many weights and biases, each is treated as an independent parameter and updated accordingly.

If you are able to understand it, great! I think you'll find this information valuable and very cornerstone to your understanding of future algorithms. If not, try your best! Any information you can get will be worth it. I'll personally recommend the YouTube channel 3Blue1Brown and his playlist series on neural networks and back-propagation; I've always loved his visual and pragmatic approach to teaching.

One whole classification of artificial intelligence that wasn't covered at all in this book is the contemporary idea of generative artificial intelligence, or artificial intelligence that can produce its own, new data based on existing data patterns and data samples. This is the most promising development in the entire tech industry; if we can learn to control and regulate generative AI, the possibilities are endless for what it can do to make our world a better place.

Now, the most common type of generative artificial intelligence is an architecture known as the large language model (LLM). I guarantee you're familiar with a couple of these LLMs: ChatGPT from OpenAI, Gemini from Google, among others. Every major tech company has their own spin on the idea of an LLM, and if you've ever used one, you know how powerful they are with text summarization, creation, etc.

The possibilities with these LLMs are endless, and they only get more powerful as they are trained on more data (us humans!) but also external resource databases. Like always, I'll encourage you to investigate the underlying mechanism behind these large language models, which is something called transformer architecture.

First invented by Google and published in their paper "Attention Is All You Need." In short, transformer architecture is a highly sophisticated natural language processing system which is able to take in text input and produce text as an output. Transformers take in words and convert them into numerical representations which are known as embeddings. The model then uses something called "self-attention"; essentially, the model takes all of the words in the input and determines which other words outside of the input are necessary for a clear understanding of the input words themselves. This self-attention process is highly complex; it involves many layers, and repetitive self-attention mechanisms to help the language model learn complex patterns within the data, which are then outputted into numerical embeddings that can be used to predict the next word in a sequence. This is how LLMs work: simply predicting the next word intelligently.

Now, that is just one transformer, but LLMs have multiple layers of these transformers themselves that are able to take in complex data as input and output a detailed and intricate response. GPT and other LLMs are trained on huge datasets; as a result, they have a wide pool of information to turn to and can therefore make incredibly complex judgements.

The scaling up of LLMs and the possible creation of new, more advanced architectures capable of natural language processing; it's great to get on the jump now and learn about these technologies before they eventually become obsolete. Besides, ChatGPT is the most popular AI tool in the world as of writing this; learning its inner working can give you the upper edge in technical conversations, or simply feed your desire for knowledge by giving you a complex challenge and forcing you to learn its inner workings.

Another common generative artificial intelligence system is more generic, but I believe its applicable in a lot more use cases. And, contrary to transformer architecture and LLMs, this next architecture is relatively intuitive. It's name: generative adversarial networks or GANs.

If you're familiar with game theory, GANs work in something known as a zero-sum game, where the gain of another player must result in an equivalent loss of another, leading to a total sum of zero. This concept is applied into neural networks, where there are two networks engaged in a zero-sum game.

A GAN consists of two different neural networks: the generator and the discriminator. In traditional GANs, the generator network initially takes random input and converts it into the output format that is needed (typically an image; 28 x 28 pixel image), and the discriminator network is given the generated image and a real sample, and is supposed to make a decision one which one is the real image. As a result of this process, both of these neural networks learn something, which they can use to gradient-descent, and back-propagate their way into make their performance greater. As a result of intensive training, both of these neural networks are honed to be able to generate and discriminate data as strong as possible.

Here's an image that may make the process easier to visualize:

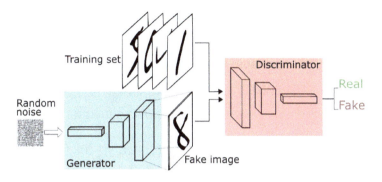

Figure 13: Generative Adversarial Network

Now, this makes the GAN a double-edged sword; one the one hand, you can focus training into the generator so you can generate high-quality images of whatever data you desire, but you can alternatively train a detailed discriminator which can not only detect fake images but also differentiate between the types of images themselves. Although the former is more common in GAN use cases, both are used often in practical applications of the GAN.

Speaking of it's applications, the GAN has seen the rise of a lot of different use cases, many more that the transformer architecture implemented in LLMs. Common ones include:

- Image (face) generation and deepfake generation by leveraging the generator.

- Super resolution of images; scaling up the resolution of images that are low-resolution by using the generator's image generation capabilities.

- Music and audio synthesis.

- Medical applications where medical images are generated synthetically in the case of scarce patient data and for patient safety and security.

- Style transfer: switching artistic styles (i.e. a painting) into a another medium (i.e. a photograph); this can create hyper-realized artistic images.

Now, those are just some of the common applications of GANs; in reality, they can be used for almost any use case imaginable. That's why I think they're objectively more relevant than transformer architecture; although the latter is powerful, it is likely to be replaced due to its nicheness, which is not a problem that GANs are likely to suffer from. They can be applied into the medical field, computer science, cybersecurity, law, among others. The true variety that GANs bring to the table in terms of the types of problems that they can handle is truly remarkable, which is why I believe that they should be something of value for you to study.

Mind you, the concepts that GANs use aren't new; it's just a combination of neural networks and game theory in a clever way to give the feeling of generative

AI by generating new content progressively.

If we're talking purely mathematics for a minute, one field which you'll find more valuable that calculus (single variable or multivariate) is linear algebra, which has deeply-rooted applications with machine learning and AI, but also within the entire field of computer science as a whole. Particularly in the fields of data manipulation and management, graphics, vectoring, etc., linear algebra is applicable in almost every field imaginable. Key mathematical constructs within linear algebra like matrices, vectors, etc. have applications in many algorithms across computer science.

Super early on in this book we discussed linear regression as a fundamental supervised learning algorithm, where multiple quantitative parameters can be used to create an estimate of a new data point. That fundamental algorithm itself uses the basics of statistics and linear algebra. Matrices can be used to represents the input data and the weights and biases of neural networks, be used for dimensionality reduction, among lots of other use cases.

All higher-dimensional data can be represented with linear algebra constructs like vectors and matrices, which is what makes it so popular and useful in computer science and particularly in artificial intelligence.

A lot of the things we represented with variables in the earlier chapters (Q-tables, hyperparameters, etc.) can also be represented with linear algebra constructs, which is just another thing to keep in mind when I tell you to learn this valuable mathematical field.

I've noticed that a large amount of statistical knowledge often pairs well with not only linear algebra but also with an understanding of artificial intelligence in general. The main way that I've noticed statistics being directly applied into our use case is through a whole new field related to reinforcement learning known as Markov Chain Monte Carlo (MCMC) algorithms.

MCMC algorithms combines a statistical structure known as a Markov Chain which is used to make stochastic decisions and random sampling using something called Monte Carlo simulations. These two concepts are vital to a deeper understanding of reinforcement learning, and their combination with MCMC algorithms can enhance these algorithms themselves. Some common MCMC algorithms which you might find interesting to research are the Metropolis-Hastings Theorem and Gibbs sampling, to name a few. I'll give you a practical example of how an MCMC algorithm can be used to enhance Q-Learning. We know that Q-Learning uses direct experiences to influence its decision making via its inherent policy with Q-values. However, this can be inefficient if we stay in areas where there is little promise of reward; what if we were to instead to sample experiences directly from high-reward areas and have the agent gravitate to those locations?

Now, that's just one example, but MCMC algorithms can be seen all over, and I think you'll find studying into them to be incredibly valuable.

Okay, those are the topics which I think will greatly improve your intellectual development and growth in the fields of artificial intelligence, machine learning, and computer science in general. Again, I would like to wholeheartedly thank you for choosing to purchase and read through this book; it really does mean a lot that you would choose to read from an upcoming author who is passionate about computer science and artificial intelligence.

I plan to write other books on similar books that focus on the intersection of math and computer science, and I hope you'll find those books interesting as well as I myself become more educated on these topics for the hope that I can educate others in the process. Although the topic I'll cover will likely be niche, I want to relate it to a broader topic so that it can resonate better within broader fields.

Once again, thank you so much for reading!

www.ingramcontent.com/pod-product-compliance
Lightning Source LLC
LaVergne TN
LVHW051737050326
832903LV00023B/973